New

Monika Knotts

BookLeaf Publishing

Presentation by *BookLeaf Publishing*

Web: www.bookleafpub.com

E-mail: info@bookleafpub.com

ISBN: 9789357442442

First edition 2023

Shoutout to my roommate and The Churb.

Day 18

the train was delayed today
things are always changing

I forgot you can ask
what places are good
I forgot other people
are living

I forgot to call my grandparents
again
but I know they will
forgive me

Day 19

I try not to think about it
how abnormal it is in
my life

when he
speaks gently and
when he
forgives.

He asks why
it takes so long
to ask

I say I'm bracing for
what daggers may come
he offers me
something else,

a haven
a softness
a question I wasn't expecting

I try not to think about it.
It makes me feel
too big for
my skin.

Day 20

Come back to me in April
when thoughts can bloom
and suffocating snowstorms
have passed

For now, leave me
in my cave
warm and bundled
so I reemerge enthused

again with the idea of living.
These little cycles
feel absurdly human and
I imagine breaking free

but I am, unfortunately,
absurdly human
hibernation is frowned upon
and grounds for eviction.

Day 21

I am real in
your eyes, and still
adored and I
only now realize it's possible

It sounds mundane,
our love. Because it is
every small and sacred thing
we touch

Day 22

I'm here to ride out the end
of the world, to do
as the Romans do
or have done
eating drinking dancing
fucking up and
down the hall to my
tiny apartment
an oasis in a cold desert
for the low low price of
my endless labor

But I'll live as long as
any of us do
here is the best of humanity
alas, hell is other people
but we do our best
to keep warm in the
wrath of eternity
each wondering what it's worth
when eternity comes to a screeching
halt, 90 seconds to midnight
that's all

Day 23

Hello, it's retrospect
coming at you from day
34 upon realizing this
page was blank

It's not been that long
but all I'll say is
it ain't so bad
just keeps going

Day 24

I noticed an object that
had fallen off its shelf
only to be caught by
a neighboring shelf that was leaned
so slightly
due to uneven distribution of
weight.

I feel like that today and
most of the time,
an accident being held
in this space
by miraculous mundane
circumstance

consciousness is
damned
good thing time seems
linear. does it?
because my dreams take me
back and forward and elsewhere
and still, there is no relief

hard to imagine a
suspended object
fearing it's eventual
retrieval

Day 25

it's kind of silly
like skipping cracks in
sidewalks
or holding your
breath in cemeteries

twice a day
the clock reads 12:34
I'm reminded
I can only go forward
maddening consecutiveness

one before two before
any thing else
sort of comforting like
listening to hold music
an undeterminable between

sometimes I forget
the marching on of things
twice a day I am reminded
from another dimension
that I am here now

Day 26

I cried this morning
for the first time in years
when pants that claimed
to be mine
refused to zip up

there I was, grown but still
12 and embarrassed
gripping baby fat in
fluorescent dressing rooms
wishing to be thin enough
to disappear

Day 27

I cry about lots of things
lately it's love love love
never demolished the pedestal

ours isn't balconies and
confessions in the night
it goes out in broad daylight

says good morning to passersby
remembers to remind me
to eat and take vitamins

on this plane together
souls wandering, being found
being seen, being made real

I cry about a lot of things
love love love
in sure daylight

Day 28

maybe life is too good
to write good poetry

in a home with more
love than i thought possible

in a city i daydreamed
since childhood into life

the things i take pills for
feel out of place

Day 29

it's unsettling
living like this
i don't get to choose
which things will
send me spiraling into
incapacity

i pick a new thing,
sometimes to ruin my own day
or days and weeks
and i'm not sure antipsychotics
do anything at all

tomorrow i'll decide
that my skin is too tight
and the inability to remove it
will render me paralyzed

does any of it matter?
objectively, no. but
that doesn't matter

and why don't we shove ice
picks into frontal lobes anymore?

sounds like the vacation of a lifetime

Day 30

the problem is,
they're all still here
like a russian doll
every version tucked away
inside this incredulous woman

I feel so silly
big girls don't cry
but I am still small
somewhere, defenseless
grown ups don't wallow

but conjured so easily
teenage feelings, grounded rage
kindergarten time out seething
they sit in my throat
like swallowing rocks

pressure builds
nested voices scream
once upon a time, release
was scratching, starving,
sex and faceless men

I've learned to be still
but the urge to purge

past from present
is never fully satiated
a perpetual gnawing

guilt they call it
shame, i could've done
so much without it
but this loathing of self
is an heirloom

quietly passed
and passed and passed
gnawing gnawing
like lipstick tarnished teeth
on freshman year nails

is it weak to feed it
sometimes, sins exchanged
for peace? it'll pass
one moment or many
I can swallow rocks smiling

I don't want to seem healed

the breaks are clean and final
but this moment might
lead to another, maybe
one that would render
screaming silent, awe-full

Day 31

I'm scared I'll run out
always closer than
I'll let myself believe

a convenient mindset
grind grind grind
the machine's poorly oiled

fear drives me
drops me off, tells me
to have a good day

but it's not enough
hopelessness cuts the brakes
renders me bedridden

is there a world where
circumstance and ruthlessness
are irrelevant in deciding

who is worthy
and who will starve
and who will turn away

I'm scared I'll run out
nothing with nothing
ground to a fine dust

Day 32

a lifetime of reality checks
and rugs pulled from underneath
will confuse your guts

people don't always say
what they mean
I can't seem to hold it in

devotion and desperation
please love me
there's no other reason

there's a trapdoor waiting
under my feet,
tell me I'm wrong, forever

Day 33

I'm amazed at the finity
living anywhere else, a city
like this is the world

but here, living, you find
there is an end
and I wonder what we're looking for

those who come seeking
and what to do when it's unfindable
where else to go

all reaching
making ourselves big
trying to touch the edge

Day 34

a dull pain in my temple
was it dumb to move here?
maybe, but what else is there
to do?

money, money, money
millions of nothings
made up to keep us
at someone's mercy

ground to the bone
scraping the bottom like
subway rails scrape
might as well

have moved here, then.
millions of nothings
float in the air, I can
have them if I

type the right words
flash the right smiles
at the right men
who think i'm the right kind

of pretty and smart
the kind that leaves them
in their places, and me
in mine

Day 35

some days pass peacefully
more often now than ever
and their unremarkability
dazzles me endlessly

grocery shopping and housework
smoking a joint before dinner
and after
sitting quietly in the company

of the life I've built
through hell and high water
hard to believe I
made it home

Day 36

mold it, shape it
with your hands
imagine what it could be

when things become rigid
douse in the water that made you
remember it's not so serious

holes drilled in
freshly painted walls
nothing gold can stay

Day 37

what is childhood
to a girl?
short and sour

the whiplash of womanhood
can come about
at any age

what am I if not
an object of desire?
learn to be small

passive and quiet
but loud to enough to assure
him, he's a big man

a wife will never be
the same thing they were
before, a loss of sheen

a wearing down
she's tired, so are you
go to bed

feel big for a moment
she'll play coy
feel shiny and new

Day 38

The mean reds
in New York City
it's true you're always there
when you leave

second chances exist
in the spaces between
what are you going to be?
quick

I don't know how
many chances I'll have,
hard to count
things are always changing

doesn't make sense
to want when wanter's
needs are met
go to work

don't look up until
there's something to see
get some rest, there's
a long life ahead

www.ingramcontent.com/pod-product-compliance
Lightning Source LLC
LaVergne TN
LVHW021351200726
843509LV00014B/2786